How To Live Happily Ever After

12 Things You Can Do to Live Forever

Lindsay Collier

January 2015

Table of Contents

Appendix One - Happy Words

Appendix Two - Some Titles You May Want to Give
Yourself

Appendix Three - Quotations to Tickle Your Brain

Appendix Four - Tips for Being Creative

Appendix Five - A Few Dumb Things You Can Do

Appendix Six - Interesting Facts to Stimulate
Your Thinking

How to Live Happily Ever After

Introduction

"It takes a long time to grow young."

This booklet contains some very different ideas on how to live forever. It even comes with a money-back guarantee. If this doesn't result in your living forever, your money will be cheerfully refunded. I've spent most of my life studying how people can be more creative in their personal and work lives, and the following is my attempt to apply some of these ideas to happily attaining longevity. We are all different, and some of these may not be suitable to you for various reasons. And, there will be some ideas that won't be entirely new to you. But there are also many ideas here that are very new and different, great fun, and highly creative. A few of them may even seem a bit weird at first. But sometimes you really need to venture on to the "roads less traveled" to find those life changing experiences. As they say, "If you always use the same ingredients, you'll always get the same bread". Although these ideas are mainly meant for those of us in our "mature years", they really apply to you no matter what your age.

One of the overriding things to keep in mind as you grow older (or throughout your life for that matter) is what Earl Nightingale calls the secret to life:

You are what you think!

Another way of putting this is that "we are what we think about". If you think about yourself as being old, then guess what? You will feel old, act old, and do things that will support that negative feeling. If you think of yourself as still young, or even just "nicely matured", then there is a good chance that you are putting yourself in a position to act that way. Is the glass half full or half empty is an old cliché, but it's still a great one to keep in mind here. The ideas that follow will help you grow old (or maybe I should say *grow young*) in style, but they will work far better if you have a positive view that you are, in fact, still young and in the "half full glass" phase of your life.

Some other things to keep in mind are embodied in theses quotations:

"Old age is like flying a plane through a storm. Once you're aboard, there's nothing you can do."

I don't believe this! There are lots of things you can do while on board in your life to extend it and make it much happier, and that's what I want to share with you in this booklet.

"Don't take life too seriously; you'll never get out of it alive."

I think we all take things too seriously much of the time. Sometimes we just need to loosen up and let life flow. Consider the following and see if this helps you to loosen up a bit:

The nucleus accounts for almost all the atom's solidarity yet occupies one million millionth of its total volume. The rest is empty space (with electrons spinning around). Bodies are mostly empty space. The solid matter for all the human bodies on earth lumped together would be no bigger than a pea. The solid matter for the entire world would fit inside a football stadium.

Now – do you feel better and less serious about this whole thing knowing that you are really just a lot of empty space?

My wife, Jean, and I live in a wonderful retirement community in Central Florida called The Villages (even though I will never admit to being retired). The majority of the residents there have a great outlook on life. We sometimes refer to The Villages as "God's Waiting Room." And those who live there year round call themselves "Frogs" as in "I'm here till I

6

croak." The majority of residents are very active, physically and mentally. There are over 2000 clubs to choose from touching every subject imaginable. There is even a club that calls itself "The Villages Idiots" that claims to have no redeemable value whatsoever. Golf is king here but there are many other sporting activities to choose from. And there is a College of Continued Learning that offers hundreds of courses to keep those aging brain cells percolating. The most popular saying there is, "It is what it is." Keep that saying in your mind, and use it whenever you can.

I spent the majority of my life as an engineer for a major company (Eastman Kodak in the good old days) followed by a period of consulting, writing, and speaking. My expertise and my speaking and writing topics revolved around creativity and innovation in your life and work. I wrote 3 books, **The Whack-A-Mole Theory**, **Get Out of Your Thinking Box**, and **Quotations to Tickle Your Brain** that were mainly aimed at creativity, innovation, and breakthrough in groups and organizations. My fourth book, **Organizational Mental Floss; How to Squeeze Your Organization's Thinking Juices**, was 75% complete when I lost my wife of 40 years to ovarian cancer. I am happy to say that I have now published that book. My process of healing from this terrible loss was greatly enhanced by the writing of my 5th book, **Surviving the Loss of Your Loved One; Jan's Rainbow**. In this book, I used some of my knowledge of creative thinking to develop ideas to help others recover from similar losses. The inspiration came from a rainbow that surrounded our home after her death. I teamed up with 28 other authors who told their stories about how their loved ones had communicated with them. I believe this book has helped hundreds of people in coping with loss, and that makes me feel great! It also contributed a great deal to my own healing.

In **How to Live Happily Ever After** my goal is to lay out some creative ideas for growing old in style. Let's start by changing that to **growing young** in style. I hope you will have a few laughs, get some great new ideas, and incorporate them into your own lives. So loosen up and fasten your seat belts and enjoy the ride!

I've grouped these ideas into 12 fairly short chapters. At the end of each chapter I've included some key questions for you to explore to help you expand your own thinking in each area. A very good friend of mine has a men's discussion group, and has used the ideas in this book to form his topics for discussion. I invite you to also give this a try. I realize that you will be tempted to just gloss over these questions and go on to the next chapter, but please don't. Answer these questions as best you can before moving on. And then when you finish the book, expand on your answers. The model that I find useful is to write down the first answers that come to mind. Then at a later time go through and expand your answers. This will help you take advantage of what I call **creative marination**. Your original thoughts will hang around in your head, some interim thoughts will connect to them, and when you go back to the question there will be some more brain fodder to help you expand your thinking on the question.

And there is one more point I'd like to make. I've done a tremendous amount of reading in my life. And I've noticed that a lot of books tend to contain a lot of "fluff". I feel your time is important and that you don't need the fluff, so I apply some "anti-fluffinator" to all my writing. I take a few side trips here and there but always ask the question, "Will this add value to reader's experience?" and, if not, it gets canned. Enjoy!

Chapter 1

Finding Your Reason for Being – What Makes You Essential

One of the most powerful books I've ever read is Victor Frankl's, **Man's Search for Meaning**, published in 1946. Frankl was a Jewish psychiatrist who was imprisoned in Nazi Germany. He decided that while he was there he would study the psychiatry of a concentration camp, and he found that those who tended to survive this ordeal were not always the strong and young as you might expect. The survivors tended to be those who had **something significant in their lives to complete**. This is a huge lesson in surviving the most difficult challenges in our lives. There is also another very powerful message from this. When you are put into a bad situation, you should take on a mindset that says, "How can I make the best of this?" as Frankl did.

So what does make you essential? Who are the people that rely on you? What are the skills that you have, and can build on? What are your goals in life? What are the things in your life you have left to do? When I lost my wife, Jan, I decided that my extensive knowledge in creative thinking could be put to use to help others cope with loss in their life. And now I'm using these same ideas to help people grow older in style.

You don't think anything makes you essential? Think again. Write down all the possibilities and expand on them. These don't have to be things that change the world, just things that help you realize that you are important and maybe play a major role in the lives of your friends, family, and others. And remember, as someone once said,

"If you think you're too small to make a difference then you've never been in bed with a mosquito."

To really expand your thinking in this area, start your own company and hire yourself on as President and CEO. Here's your chance to have that great title! You may even want to create a business card to hand out to your friends and family. Your company could be **Me Inc.** and you can give yourself any title you want. Better still, give your company a really creative name! Here are a few possibilities for your title. See the Appendix 2 for a longer list.

Raging Inexorable Thunder-Lizard Creativity Evangelist
All That Is Powerful and Wise
Big Kahuna
Director of Fun
Master of Madness
Pride Piper of Creativity
Wicked Good Idea Generator
Idea Gooser
Wizard of Wonder
Hope Builder
Cerebral Proctologist (I think I may have lost a few customers when I carried this title)
Chief Imagination Officer
Human Being
Director of Everything
Chief Humor Officer
Squeezer of Organizational Thinking Juices
Manager of Mischief
Rocker of Boats

Feel free to use any of these or, better still, invent your own title, one that really turns you on and excites you. Use any of these titles as stepping stones to create your own. And you don't have to keep the same title forever. Change to a new title whenever you want – remember you are your own boss.

Finding out what makes you essential creates a powerful incentive to lead you on the way to a long, happy life. Spend some time on the following questions before going on to the next chapter. Answer these as best you can right now – you will have an opportunity to expand on them later.

Questions for Chapter 1

Think about the statement, "You are what you think".

What do you think of yourself?

What do you think of your future?

What to you think of your capabilities?

What do you think about your importance to others?

What makes you essential?

What are the significant things you have left to do in your life?

Who are the people who most influenced you? In what ways did they influence you?

Who would say are the people you most influence?

What are the significant things you have accomplished in your lifetime and how might you add to these?

Chapter 2

Focusing on the Positive

"The winner sees a green near every sand trap. The loser sees a sand trap near every green."

In my observations of people through the years I have noticed that too many people tend to focus on all the reasons why things *can't be* done. As someone once said, *"Where there's a will there's a won't"*. And then there are those of us who focus on how things *can be* done. I've always tried my best to be one of them – and you should too. I realize of course that there is a continuum here, and most people's thinking doesn't occur on either end but somewhere between the two extremes. I've come to believe that the norm tends to be further towards the "can't be" end and, when the focus is on the reasons why things can't be done, it is likely nothing will get done.

I'm reminded of a story I heard quite a while ago that has rather stuck with me through the years:

> *It was Christmas and a little boy and girl were very excited to see what Santa had left so they snuck down a little early to take a peak. The only thing they saw was a huge pile of manure next to the tree. The little boy ran back to his room crying thinking that he must have behaved very badly to deserve this. The little girl ran to the woodshed to get a shovel, came back and began shoveling like mad saying. "There must be a pony in here somewhere."*

Now this may not be the most exciting analogy, but sometimes I think you need to shovel a little manure out of the way if you want to find the things you want in your life.

If you can focus on how things "can be done" there is a much higher probability that you will get results. This concept seems rather simple but I must stress how important it is for carrying out most of the suggestions in this booklet. In my creative problem solving consulting I often used a technique from my friend, Sidney Shore, called, "What's good about it?" When you encounter a problem, focus on the things that are good about that problem and use these things to help solve the problem. It may surprise you to learn that there are always more positive aspects of a negative situation than you thought there were. And this will push you into focusing on the positive.

If you think you may be one of those who lean toward a negative focus you may have to work on moving to the positive side. Try it out on the next few problems or decision points you encounter. This may be a bit uncomfortable at first, but push as hard as you can into a positive focus. Enlist the help of someone close to you if necessary. Once you are able to regularly focus on the positive you'll be a much happier, more productive person. And, if you have some friends or associates that tend toward the negative, try to push them to the positive. In doing this you will also strengthen your own ability to stay positive.

It's important to note that the words you use have an impact upon your ability to focus on the positive. If you use positive words you will find it much easier to have a positive outlook. If you use negative words you may find it difficult to stray from negative thought. Think about the words you tend to use. Track them for a while if you can. Do you lean towards positive or negative words? If you lean towards the negative, make a concerted effort to add more positive words to your vocabulary. It will definitely change your outlook!

Some of my friends consider me to be the ultimate optimist. One of my inspirations comes from an article I found in the newspaper years ago about Les Paul, the guitar genius. Here are some highlights from that article that should also inspire you to focus on the positive:

When Paul performs on the electric guitar it's hard to believe that acute arthritis has immobilized all the fingers of his right hand and crippled all but two fingers on his left, or fingerboard, hand. "I had to learn to play the guitar all over again as the arthritis got worse," Paul says. "I play real good now with just two fingers."

Paul also suffers from the effects of a 1948 automobile accident where he suffered a broken back, fractured pelvis, broken collarbone, broken ribs, a ruptured spleen, and a right arm that was so crushed there was talk of amputating it. Doctors managed to reconstruct his arm and set it pointed at his navel, in a guitar-playing position. "It won't move but I can still hold a guitar," Paul says with a laugh.

He has also been through bone-graft surgery on his left hand; he has suffered from sciatica and Meniere's disease; he has had three operations on his right ear to correct a broken eardrum; and has had a quintuple heart bypass. Nevertheless, Paul has managed to put a positive spin on his misfortunes.

"With every setback, every hospitalization, I've done some creating," he says. "If you can't play, you can think, you can sit there and invent. So when someone tells me I've had a lot of hardships I tell them that a lot of good things have come from them."

If that story doesn't inspire you to be an optimist nothing will! By the way, I've noticed that *Optimist's Clubs* are popping up in a number of places (such as where I live in The Villages, Florida). If there is one near you consider joining it.

Here are a couple more stories that should help you on the path towards becoming a more positively focused person:

The Grandfather Story

Many years ago, a young man and his grandfather spent their days together, as was the custom. The old man spent much time teaching the boy how to hunt, fish, and make things, and to do it all in a sacred way. Having lived many years, the grandfather possessed many great powers of healing and teaching. Great was his knowledge of many things. One day the grandfather said to the boy, "We will change the course of the mighty river."

The boy was filled with wonder, for he knew that his grandfather was a great man and could do great things. But change the course of a great river? Who of mortal man could accomplish such a great deed?

As they approached the river, the boy's heart leapt as he imagined the course of the river being changed. When they got to the bank of the river, the old man reached down into the river and picked out a rock about the size of a melon.

The boy watched as the hole that the rock left began to fill with water, and he understood that in some small way the old man had indeed changed the course of the mighty river.

The old man looked at the boy with a twinkle in his eye and said, "This is the way the great river is changed, one rock at a time. It is the duty of every man who walks to change the course of rivers. Every action that you do, every word that you say will affect or change the course of a person's life. Keep on changing the course of rivers, little one." Grandfather was a wise man.

The Starfish Story

A young man is walking along the ocean and sees a beach on which thousands and thousands of starfish have washed ashore. Further along he sees an old man, walking slowly and stooping often, picking up one starfish after another and tossing each one gently into the ocean.

"Why are you throwing starfish into the ocean?" he asks.

"Because the sun is up and the tide is going out

and if I don't throw them further in they will die."

"But, old man, don't you realize there are miles and miles of beach and starfish all along it!

You can't possibly save them all, you can't even save one-tenth of them. In fact, even if you work all day, your efforts won't make any difference at all."

The old man listened calmly and then bent down to pick up another starfish and threw it into the sea. "It made a difference to that one."

Questions for Chapter 2

Where do you honestly see yourself on the scale between positive and negative outlook?

How do some of your best friends and family members see you on that scale?

Do you tend to use positive words in your conversation with others?

What are the characteristics of the situations you see as negative?

Think of a neutral to negative situation that you are currently facing and should take some action on. What is good about it?

Is there someone you could discuss this with who might help you find a more positive outlook toward it?

Can you rephrase the wording of some situations so they become more positive?

Chapter 3

Taking Care of Your Body and Your Mind; Physical/Mental Workouts and Eating Habits

It's no secret that our bodies and our minds need to be active to stay healthy. We all have different circumstances regarding our ability to stretch ourselves physically and mentally. And, let's face it, we have probably lost our chance to be in the Olympics, or graduate with honors from a distinguished university. So we need to stretch our minds and bodies just enough to keep them "well oiled". And it's important to note that there is a strong supportive connection between our bodies and our minds. Physical activity elevates mental acuity. The *hippocampus* is a curved ridge of tissue in each cerebral hemisphere of the brain concerned with basic drives, emotions, and short-term memory. Research shows that physical and mental activities both go a long way towards enhancing this tissue. So the next time someone asks you what you are doing as you carry out your physical and mental exercises tell them, "I'm building up my hippocampus". They will be either very impressed or think you are really losing it.

Physical Workouts

As far as physical workouts, do as much as you think you can – and then stretch it just a bit further. It's usually most beneficial when you stretch yourself to a point just beyond your comfort level. If walking is your thing, then try to walk just a little longer or a little faster each day. You probably don't want to participate in physical workouts that tax your joints too much. Walking is one of the single best and easiest options that will keep you active without overdoing it. Swimming and biking are great too, and participating in sports like golf, pickle ball, tennis etc is always good. If you are a gardener that is sometimes the best work out of all. Remember, the idea is to keep your body active, not to create *Abs of steel.* Your dreams of these abs may be long gone. It sometimes takes a bit of disciplining to force yourself to do some of these things. The older we are the easier it is to make a lot of excuses for not exercising. Believe me; I've used every excuse in the book myself at one time.

It's very important to have a periodic (at least yearly) physical. A lot of physical problems when caught early can be eliminated. I believe most health care plans cover annual physicals with no co pays so there is no excuse for not doing this. The medical profession has come a long way in developing the capability to computerize and track information on patients so any problems can be dealt with early. Many of them offer personal websites for people to track their health issues. Blood tests reveal a plethora of information to track your health. Since cholesterol numbers are important as indicators of future problems you need to know what your various numbers are and this can get pretty confusing. Take time to learn about total cholesterol, HDL (good), LDL (bad), and triglycerides, and make sure these are all under control. Your heart will love you for it. Blood pressure is a very important thing to track as well. Get yourself a blood pressure monitor and use it at least once a week. Some testers have the ability to track your history, but I use a free App on my IPad, called *iBP,* which does a great job tracking and charting this information. Remember, high or low blood pressure can cause you a lot of problems. Knowing where you stand is important because, in most cases, it can be fairly easily controlled with medicine or other interventions such as weight control and exercise.

Mental Workouts

As far as mental workouts are concerned, there are lots of choices. Cross word puzzles, Sudoku, Words with Friends and other brain boosters are readily available. Have you noticed that the *brain booster* book sections in the most bookstores are getting bigger? Go to that section of your favorite bookstore and pick up a few of these books. There are also a number of brain booster apps and games for your IPad, smart phone or other similar device. Most of these are free but in some cases you may have to fork over a whole $.99 to get an add-free version. Choose games and puzzles that really challenge you and stretch your thinking like a rubber band – not just the ones you can easily solve. As a matter of fact, the best ones might be those that you can't quite solve. When that is the case you know you are taking yourself right to the edge. And the more you take yourself to the edge, the higher your chances are to eventually extend beyond that edge. And, like a rubber band, the more it is stretched, the more pliable it becomes. Most newspaper puzzles start on Monday with the easiest and get more difficult as the week goes on. Challenge yourself to get through the whole week with a particular puzzle. Give me a call if you get to the point of solving Saturday's puzzle and let me know what your secret is. I've never been able to come even close to solving Saturday's crossword, but maybe someday. I'll keep on trying. Also, challenge yourself to learn some brand new skills that will help you stretch your thinking while adding a little zest to your life.

A part of your mental work out should also be to read as often as you can. You may be able to find some learning possibilities on the TV, but sometimes it's just best to turn it off and open a good book or magazine. If you are a compulsive TV watcher make sure you spend some time on the learning channels. Keep a variety in your reading lists to include fiction, non-fiction, short stories, auto-biographies, history, magazines etc. And you may want to try your hand at writing too (more about this later). Most people don't look at themselves as being authors but you may surprise yourself. Once you begin writing it seems to open up the floodgates of your mind and it becomes quite addictive. And you just may find that you are smarter than you thought you were - as I did.

Eating Habits

For many of us weight tends to become a problem with age. When you were younger it didn't seem to be a problem to shave off a few pounds whenever you wanted. It's no secret that being overweight can shave some years off your life, so it's something you need to keep in mind. I tried weighwatchers.com for a while and found it to be very valuable for keeping track of the food I ate so that I could change my eating habits.

Weightwatchers can get a bit expensive but there is a very nice free App available called **_Lose It!_** which does *almost* everything that *Weightwatchers* does.

Snacking can be a big problem but according to *Weightwatchers* you can snack on fruits and veggies just about as much as you want. So the next time you feel like raiding the cookie jar, raid the fruit/veggie bowl instead. Portion control is also very important. Do you really need that 12 oz steak? Start by cutting your portion by ¼ and then work to ½. You will also find you are much more comfortable after eating smaller portions. And I'm convinced that drinking water is very beneficial to heath and weight. Google "drinking water for health" to read the many articles on this topic. Eight 8 ounce glasses per day is a good goal.

It goes almost without saying that it is very important to be aware of those habits that can be harmful. Smoking is probably the one worst habit and, if you are a smoker, you should take every possible effort to quite. I have some good friends who were lifetime smokers who quit using hypnosis. I was very impressed with how effective that was for them and how they have never returned to this habit. I smoked myself for a number of years but quite 35 years ago when I realized that it was messing up my tennis game. Obviously that was one of the best decisions I ever made. Other drugs and alcohol use can also be issues. If that is the case with you then you need to do what you can to address these issues.

Questions for Chapter 3

Thinking about your body:

What are you doing to stay physically fit? Are you stretching yourself? How?

What are some additional activities you might want to try for exercise?

Is your weight where you want it to be? What are your plans for changing this?

Thinking about your mind:

Are you doing any brain boosters? Which ones?

How often are you reading? Are you diversifying your reading?

Are you doing any writing? If not, what are some possibilities?

Thinking about your eating habits:

How is your food portion control?

Are you eating healthy foods? What might you do to make changes here?

Are you a snacker? What can you do to eliminate snacks or move to healthy snacks?

Do you have any habits that are harmful to your health? What are you going to do about them?

Chapter 4

Continuously Tapping Your Creativity

I admit, I'm rather bias about the importance of creative thinking in our lives. Early on in my career as an engineer I made an observation that has stuck with me for many years. I noticed that for the most part people tended to leave their right brains at the gate when going to work. So I began an intensive study of the field of creative thinking and became somewhat of an expert in the area of how to use creative thinking in work and personal lives. Along the way I've made hundreds of presentations on this topic and trained many to become creative process facilitators.

As we age, many of us lose our incentive to use our creative thinking capacity. The result is that we may lose one of the major sources of excitement and innovation in our everyday lives. Being able to continuously tap your creativity is an important part of living a happy and exciting life.

Creativity is often referred to as "thinking outside the box". Our thinking tends to be limited by what we see as the rules of possibility sometimes called "paradigms". The older we are, the more time we've had to build these paradigms into our thinking. Children are rarely limited in their thinking until their parents, teachers, and other various forms of elders have had a chance to orient them to the "rules". Sometimes our "fear of failure" gets in the way. We won't try something new and different because we are afraid of failing which is often considered bad. But, remember, many failures are just pathways to new opportunities. It's been said that *"everywhere you trip is an opportunity"*. So maybe you need to fail quickly so you can succeed sooner. And don't worry too much about being first with an idea. As they say, "The early bird gets the worm but the second mouse gets the cheese." So for us to tap our creativity we need to "break the rules" and here are some ways for you to do this.

Recognize Your Creative capacity - Everyone (you and me included) comes loaded with an incredible capacity for creativity. The problem is that we experience things in our lives that result in a build-up of blockages. Over time these blockages erode our self-confidence so that most people begin to believe that they are just not that creative. Ask your friends and associates if they are creative and you'll find most of them will hedge a bit, or just say no. So the first thing I want you to do is to tell yourself that you are incredible creative. Go ahead – do it now. And keep telling yourself until you really, truly believe it. And, as you convince yourself of your creative capacity don't forget to throw in the proclamation that you can really make a difference in everything in which you are involved.

Fire your judge – Most of us have tendency to scrutinize and negatively pre-judge any thoughts or ideas that are different. Much of this pre-judging comes from your associates but a major part of it comes from your own inner thinking. We are often our own worst critics! If you focus on all the reasons why a new idea *won't* work there is little possibility that it *will* work. So fire your judge and the next time you come up with the seed of an idea ask yourself, "How can I make this work?" Closely related to this thought is our fear of failure. It is often this fear that keeps us from thinking or trying new and different things. It is difficult for many of us to recognize the value of failure as Thomas Edison did when he said, "Every time I fail I've learned one more way not to achieve my goal." So, remember, most failures are just stepping stones to success.

Identify the rules and then break them – As a consultant in creative thinking in organizations I spent a lot of time helping my clients "break the rules". That was frightening to many because it is often imbued in us to "obey the rules". One of my favorite examples of this (I have lots of them) is the rule breaking that created the idea of hybrid vehicles. Years ago Audi questioned one of the basic rules of vehicle design – that a car has one engine. Breaking that relatively simple rule allowed them to think about the possibilities of having more than one engine and the hybrid idea was born. Another example is *"the Fosbury flop."* For years high jumpers thought that they had to go over the high bar feet first. Then Dick Fosbury came along and changed everything by going over head first and the bar (so to speak) was reset.

So if you are thinking of expanding your thinking in a particular subject, start by identifying what specific rules shape your thinking and then ask yourself what the possibilities would be if you were to break those rules.

Ask a lot of "what if?" questions

Asking "what if?" gives you the open door to expand your possibilities. The example I used to use in many of my talks was the question that was posed by some folks working on the issue of future highway safety quite a few years ago. They asked," What if telephone poles could just disappear when hit by a vehicle?" This gave them the opportunity to explore how to, in a sense, make that happen and the poles that we see today along highways became a reality. They don't really disappear, but do fracture at the base without doing tremendous damage to the vehicle.

Are there some things in your life that might change if you could identify some exciting "what if?" questions?

Use metaphors

Metaphors allow us to reshape our thinking about any topic, and the stranger the metaphor the more fun it is to play with. Many of the creative thinking techniques revolve around using metaphors. These help us overcome having our hands tied by the rules because, when you redefine your problem using a metaphor, the rules just go away. In my work with organizations I would often have people think of their team as a big compost pile (or other strange thing), think of how to make this compost pile thrive, and then transfer that thinking back to the reality of the situation. The results were often quite amazing because it allowed them to take a totally different viewpoint. I've been a gardener all my life and often find that gardening is a great metaphor for many things in my life. How might you apply some of the unique aspects of gardening to your life? And, thinking of your problem as an iceberg can sometimes yield some great new thinking since it gets you thinking about the large mass under the surface instead of just what is above it.

Go Mental Bunge Jumping

I have made hundreds of presentations to groups on how to enhance creativity. I think one of the most important concepts is what I call "mental bungee jumping" (MBS). We tend to expand our thinking by pushing forward from the point we are currently at. With MBS the idea is to stretch your thoughts to the absolute max, and then to bring them back to reality. In other words, come up with the most ridiculous ideas on a topic and then work back to how you might make these work. Can you see the analogy with bungee jumping? Next time you run into a problem that is just begging for a creative solution take this technique for a test drive.

Wander and Let Your Thoughts Marinate

One of my favorite T-shirts says, "All Who Wander Are Not Lost." I'm convinced that a lot of great thoughts come to mind when you just let your mind and/or body wander. Mozart once said, *"When I am, as it were, completely myself, entirely alone, and of good cheer – say traveling in a carriage, or walking after a good meal, or during the night when I cannot sleep; it is on such occasions that my ideas flow best and most abundantly."*

What were you doing the last time you had a great idea? Most people say they were taking a shower, driving, running or walking, mowing the lawn, or in some form of sleeping. People seem to do some of their best creative thinking when engaged in a somewhat *mindless* activity. So give yourself some time to wander both physically and mentally. But while you are doing this observe as much as you can and try to make connections to things that are hanging around in your head. That's where the idea of *marination* comes in. Some of our best and most creative thoughts come to us after they've had a good chance to soak in our brains

Find Your *Thinkorarium*

Glenn Curtiss, one of the most prolific inventors in the 1930's and 40s, had a cupola on top of his house overlooking one of the Finger Lakes in upstate New York. He called this his **thinkorarium** and it was where he went anytime he wanted to expand his thinking. Find a *thinkorarium* of your own (a garden spot, a comfortable chair in your music room, driving your car etc) where you can go and expand your thinking. Sometimes you just need a little of what I call *soak time* to help ideas develop fully. Let an idea mull in your mind for a period of time and there's a good chance you'll discover some new connections that will help build on it. While writing this I am working on my website which I am calling *my thinkorarium*". My goal here is to be able to share some of the things that I have learned throughout my long career helping people tap their creative potential. You can find this at lindsaycollier.weebyl.com.

And always remember that **great ideas rarely enter the mind through the mouth**. Concentrate on listening intently to others, closely observing things around you, and building on the ideas that you take in.

Questions for Chapter 4

Do you consider yourself a very creative person? How creative are you on a scale of 1-10?

Do you tend to judge yourself a lot? Do you think the fear of failure is a factor with you?

Do you always tend to go by the rules? Are there some areas in your life where you could break the rules?

What problems or opportunities in your life might you ask "what if?" questions about? Would some of these lend themselves to some *mental bungee jumping*?

Identify a few metaphors that might aid you in thinking more creatively. Include a couple of really weird ones.

How might these metaphors raise your level of thinking?

Do you give yourself time to wander? How?

When and where do you do your best thinking? What are the possibilities for creating your own *thinkorarium*?

Chapter 5

Smiling and Laughing a Lot

"Laughter is like changing a baby's diaper. It doesn't permanently solve any problems, but it makes things more acceptable for a while."

"Smile. It improves your face value."

"Seven days without laughter makes one weak."

I have long thought that our sense of humor is one of the most powerful tools we have. I did some very interesting pioneering work while at Kodak, and actually built the *Kodak Humor Room*, one of the first ever corporate humor rooms. And I have made a number of presentations to a variety of organizations on the importance of tapping humor in the workplace. Humor is one of the most valuable assets you have throughout your life, but may be especially important as you age.

One of the pioneers of the power of humor in your life was Norm Cousins. He was editor of the Saturday Review (you are dating yourself if you remember this) and was diagnosed with what he was told was a terminal disease. He wasn't ready to accept this diagnosis and decided he would surround himself with things that made him laugh. After a period of time using laughter as medicine he received a clean bill of health. He essential "laughed himself to health". His book, *Anatomy of an Illness*, is a landmark work on the connection between laughter and health. One of the stories he tells gives us a good idea how he used humor in his life:

When he was admitted to the hospital for diagnosis the nurse brought him to his room, gave him a glass of apple juice and a specimen bottle for a urine test, and said she would return in a while for his specimen. He decided he would pour the apple juice in the specimen bottle just to see what would happen. The nurse came back to get his specimen, looked at it and said, "Mr. Cousins that looks very cloudy". He took the specimen and drank it down saying, "Yes you're right, let me put this through the filters one more time."

One of the most intriguing aspects of humor deals with a "chicken vs. egg" question. Am I laughing because I'm happy or am I happy because I'm laughing? The brain has a hard time recognizing the difference between fake laughter and real laughter. So, if you can't find anything funny at the moment, just try to laugh for no reason at all. You might want to do this while you are by yourself or those around you might think you are nuts.

I well remember a keynote speaker at a humor conference, Annette Goodheart, who came on the stage and said absolutely nothing. She began with a very quiet snicker and gradually raised this to a belly laugh. The entire audience was in stitches by the end of her presentation and she never said a word! By the way, that was quite a few years ago and I still remember her name which brings up a very important point about humor. Those things that make you laugh the loudest are the ones that stay in your memory the longest.

There is a growth around the world of "laughter clubs". These were begun by a doctor from India who felt that there was a very strong connection between humor and health. Laughter clubs began meeting each morning to begin their day with laughter. In many cases the laughter was spontaneous in the same way as Annette Goodheart's. See if there is one of these clubs in your area and give it a try.

Humor should be a very positive thing but, unfortunately, I have seen it used in some very negative ways. Spontaneous humor that comes from a position of caring about people is always the best. Humor should bring

38

people together – not tear them apart. If jokes are a form of humor you use, be careful that they don't take victims or degrade something or somebody, as is often the case. And never use humor to mask your true feelings or lack of confidence.

Someone once said, *"It's never too late to have a happy childhood. Growing old is inevitable, growing up is optional."* Here are some ways to keep on tapping your sense of humor.

Keep cheerful friends

Your best friends are the ones that make you feel good. If you have some friends that don't make you feel good then try to raise their level of humor and make them smile and laugh. Turn them into friends that make you feel good. If that doesn't work, find some new friends. Always greet your friends with a smile and never leave them until you've had a few laughs together.

Look others in the face and smile

Start each morning with a "stand, breathe, and smile exercise". Get out of bed, stand up, take a deep breath and flash the biggest smile you can. Do this a few times a day and especially when things happen to you that aren't so funny. You may want to also do this just before going to bed. Do it in front of a mirror if you can or, if you have a significant other who already thinks you're half nuts, do it in front of her/him. Better still, do it with each other.

 And each day take as many opportunities as you can to look folks in the eye and smile. This will make you feel good and the other person as well. It's also a very good way of making new friends. If you have a hard time doing this then use a "smile stick". Check out the different models at smileonastick.com. While you're at it get yourself a clown nose and some "Groucho" glasses for those times when you really want to add some humor to situations (such as at meetings). Keep in mind the old song, "Make someone happy – and you'll be happy too." How true it is.

Save some "smile mindsets" and use them when needed

We've all had experiences in our lives that just automatically bring smiles to our faces. We need to store these in a place so you can bring them to the surface whenever the need arises. So when something goes wrong or you are feeling down, you can call on one of these "smile mindsets" to remind you that life can still be a barrel of laughs. For example, my son and I were watching a game show once and the host stated that the second place prize was a year's supply of *Riceroni.* This may not sound that funny to most of you, but he just could not stop laughing. This became a "smile mindset" for him and just to mention the word still has the power to brighten his day.

Try to identify a few times in your life that had a major impact on your "funny bone" and store these in one of the permanent sections of your brain. Think of these when you are feeling down and see what happens. I think you'll be pleasantly surprised.

Keep a "silly file"

There is hardly a day that goes by without some comical piece of information coming my way. Much of it these days comes from emails I get from friends but it also comes from news, reading, observation, friend's jokes etc. I file these away in my *"silly file"* and. whenever I need something to add some humor to my life, I open up this file and do some browsing. It's a great way to get you up when you are down.

I have a *silly file* folder in my desk drawer and whenever I find something that strikes me funny I put it in this file. Every so often I'll go through the file and clean it out and I always have a blast doing this. When I do this I usually try to bring the best ones to the top so that they are easily accessible. I also have a folder on my computer labeled *silly file*. Whenever I find something funny from my emails or various wanderings around the net I copy and paste it to this file. Whenever I am asked to speak to a group I usually take time to peruse this file for some good things to share with others.

And, every now and then just do some silly things. For example, one day I was in my office working on a presentation with my Golden Retriever, Molly, snuggled in her usual spot at my feet. I glanced at a local business newspaper to see a section on people who had been promoted, and decided I would promote Molly to Chief Operations Officer of my company (which consisted only of me at the time). So I wrote a nice press release and the following week there was a nice piece about Molly's promotion. In retrospect, I wish I had included a picture.

Surround yourself with things that make you smile.

Your physical environment makes a big different in how you feel. When you create a nice bright background in the areas you inhabit you will significantly improve your outlook. Bright colors, happy pictures, silly stuff, and happy reminders of the past will change the way you think.

Watch videos or YouTubes of your favorite comedians

If your humor needs a kick start and you have access to a computer, IPad (or similar device), or a smart phone, get on it and Google (or YouTube) your favorite comedian. You will be amazed at how easy it is to access a plethora of some of the funniest routines you'll ever see. Warning! This can get very addicting. The good news is that this addition will make you feel good. Just to get you started here are my two favorite routines. Google these and try not to hurt yourself laughing.

Foster Brooks Drunken Pilot

Tim Conway/Harvey Corman Dentist

Make it a point to use happy words

The words you use each day reflect a lot about your state of mind. If you use happy words, you will tend to be happy. If you use sad words, you will tend to be sad. Sounds pretty simple doesn't it? So make it a point to use as many happy words as you can. Start by keeping a mental count of words you use that are happy. If you have a tendency to use negative words try your best to strike them from your vocabulary. Here are a few happy words to get you started. There are more in Appendix 1.

Affectionate	Elated	**Lively**
Agreeable	Enjoyable	**Loved**
Altruistic	Enthusiastic	**Lovely**
Amazed	Excellent	Magnificent
Beautiful	Excited	Marvelous
Blessed	Fabulous	**Optimistic**
Blissful	Fantastic	**Perfect**
Brilliant	Friendly	**Pleased**
Bubbly	Glad	**Pleasure**
Cheerful	**Good**	Satisfied
Chipper	**Grateful**	Spectacular
Comfortable	**Great**	Superb
Confident	**Happiness**	Sweet
Content	**Happy**	Thankful
Creative	**Heavenly**	Thrilled
Delighted	**Impressed**	Wonderful
Delightful	**Joy**	
Ecstatic	**Jubilant**	

To sum it up, a friend of mine once told me you just needed to always be a "glutton for funishment." Good advice I'd say!

> "You don't stop playing because you're old; you're old because you stopped playing."

Questions for Chapter 5

Do you consider yourself a humorous person? If not how might you change this?

How often have you smiled and laughed in the past day? Who have you made smile today?

How many of your friends would you consider as happy people? Are there some of your friends who are not happy that you can make happy?

Do you have some humorous situations in your life that you can use as your *smile mindsets* ?

Do you have some material you can use to start your *silly file?*

Look around you. Are you surrounded by an environment that makes you happy? What can you do to change this?

Do you tend to use happy or sad words? How might you change this?

Chapter 6

Always Having a Long List of Things to Do

Remember one of the lessons from **Man's Search for Meaning** which is that we will never give up when there are important things left to do. So it makes sense that we need to keep a long list of things we need to accomplish (some call these *bucket lists*). As long as we have this list we need to stick around to get it done. And if you keep adding to the list you'll never complete it so you'll just have to stick around forever.

Here are some possibilities to consider. Add some of your own to these.

Places you want to go and see. Just Google "1000 places" and check out all the books and articles that come up. Here are a few places you might want to add to your list.

- Take some day trips in your area
- Visits all the museums in your area
- Check out local walking/biking trails
- Visit the best sunrise/sunset spots
- Go horseback riding
- Go kayaking
- Places you've always wanted to see (Washington DC, Grand Canyon, Scotland etc, etc)
- Take a cruise
- Go on a picnic
- Go on a retreat
- Have a second honeymoon
-

Projects you want to complete. This could include things you want to build, writing about your passions, developing the family tree, organizing family photos, creating beautiful gardens etc.

- Create scrapbooks of your family and life experiences
- Build some models
- Create some new gardens
- Remodel your home
- Create a scrapbook of all your experiences
- Write your life story
- Organize all your family pictures in albums
- Create the family tree
-

Goals you would like to achieve.

- Achieve a certain weight – maybe one that is nearly unachievable
- Create abs of steel (good luck)
- Run a marathon or triathlon
- Shoot your age at golf (I will really have to live forever to achieve that goal)
- See your great grandkids graduate from college
- Own an exotic car
- Become an author

Totally different things you want to try

- Become a volunteer (Big Brother/Sister, hospice, hospital etc.)
- Learn to play an instrument
- Start a business
- Learn a new languag

- Learn sign language
- Become an archer
- Learn some new games
- Get a job at something that always interested you
- Start a club
- Swim with the Manatee or Dolphins
- Publish a book
- Become speaker
-

Things you want to learn.

- Learn about astronomy (Get a telescope and study the sky at night)
- Learn all you can about world wars
- Study world religions
- Become an expert in local history
- Wander Wikipedia and learn at least one new thing each day
- Read some books on topics you never thought would interest you
- Become a really good cook
- Learn various dances

Relationships you want to create or stimulate

- Contact all your friends from the past
- Connect with all your nieces, nephews, cousins, aunts/uncles
- Get reacquainted with your high school buddies
- Find your military service buddies
- Communicate with your past teachers

- Make a difference in someone's life
- Carry out acts of kindness
- Make friends with some total strangers
- Create as many friends as you can on your favorite social networks (Facebook, LinkedIn, Google+, Twitter etc)
- Go on a romantic getaway
- Fall in love or fall back in love with your spouse, partner, children etc
- Make friends with some of your past enemies
-

I'm always keeping various lists and one of the things that make me feel good is when I do something that is not on my list, I add it to my list, and then cross it off. And never be afraid to procrastinate because the more you do the longer it'll take you to complete your list. And if you decide to include completion dates on your list be sure to include *"when Hell freezes over* "or *"when pigs fly"* as one of your choices.

Questions for Chapter 6

What have you always wanted to do but haven't done yet?

What places would you like to visit if you had the time and money?

What are some things you'd like to achieve before you die? What goals would you like to achieve?

In what areas would you like to be known as an expert? What skills would you like to learn?

What projects would you like to complete?

What relationships in your life would you like to maximize?

What are your biggest dreams in life?

Chapter 7

Writing Your Life Story

Writing a life story can be a great experience. I worked almost a year on mine and enjoyed every minute of it. Initially I did it because I thought my children, and grandchildren, would like to know what it was like in the generation before them. I sure would have loved it if I could have read some life stories of my parents and grandparents. When you leave this earth all of your history goes with you unless you take the time to leave some here. I think that is one of the key reasons why I am so addicted to writing. I've lived a pretty interesting life and been able to amass a pretty good base of knowledge in a number of areas. Why should I take this with me without sharing it first with as many people as I can?

I started by going back as far as I could remember and sort of rambling forward from there. But I found that the more I brought out from my active memory bank, the more I was able to dig deeper into my memory and remember things that I had long ago forgotten. This was a great learning experience for me. Reliving most of my experiences was fun. Reliving some of the more tragic experiences sometimes brought tears to my eyes but, in the end, made me feel like I had unloaded some baggage and that's always a good thing. Based on my experience here are a few tips on how to create your life story.

Start by separating your life into different eras that represent the parts of your life that were most important. I separated mine into:

- o   The early years
- o   High school years
- o   College years
- o   Marriage and Beginning a Family
- o   My Army Years

- o   My Career with Kodak
- o   Building a Home and Growing a Family
- o   Early Retirement and a New Career
- o   Loss of my wife – Jan
- o   My Second Chance at Love – Jean
- o   Where I am Now

For each of these eras I began by brainstorming the events that came to mind. I then repeated this process several times until I couldn't think of anything else to enter. That gave me a good starting point to begin embellishing my thoughts for each of the categories. This was a wonderful experience because, the more I wrote, the more great thoughts from the past came to mind.

And then to spice things up a bit I added newsflashes from certain key turning points in my life (when I was born, graduations, military service, building a home etc.). Doing this was a blast! For example here is the newsflash for the year I was born. You can easily find this information at various websites such as http://www.thepeoplehistory.com/ .

Newsflash! It's 1941. Franklin Delanor Roosevelt is president. The war in Europe is dominating world affairs. On December 7th the US is attacked by the Japanese in Pearl Harbor and we enter into WW2. The average cost of a house is $4,075, average wages are $1750 per year, a gallon of gas is 12 cents, average price of a new car is $850, and average house rent is $32 per month. Mount Rushmore is completed and a bill is passed to make the 4th Thursday in November Thanksgiving Day. On my birthday the Boston Bruins sweep the Detroit Redwngs to win the Stanley Cup.

I also included lots of pictures in the story. I spent hours digitizing pictures from my childhood days going back to my great grandparents in the 1800's who I never even knew (I'm not that old!). The pictures really make the story interesting and the process of going through and scanning them was an experience in itself. During this process I was able to gain a lot of information for building my family tree. Working on your family tree is something you may want to consider along with writing your life story. There is some nice family tree software available and ancestry.com is a wonderful source of information.

I concluded by sharing my philosophy on life and a summary of some of the things that are important to me including:

- o The high points of my life
- o The low points of my life
- o My favorite songs
- o All of the cars I have owned
- o All of the Presidents during my years (along with a brief impression of each one)
- o Our family pets
- o My religious and political beliefs

I didn't have the luxury of having family members that I could talk with who could add some ideas since my whole family has passed. But I would suggest that you interact with as many members of your family as you can to get their input. If you have some family members that are along in years do it while you have the chance. My experience is that for the most part they love to share this information.

You may also want to have yearly updates and leave an open chapter or two. I'm thinking of a chapter called my hundredth birthday and perhaps one about my second millennium. Yes – it's good to be an optimist! Have fun!

Questions for Chapter 7

How far back in your life does your memory take you?

What are the key eras of your life?

What are the topics that come to mind within each era?

What are some of the others things you would like to share with your family and friends?

Do you have some old family photos that can be digitized to help tell your story?

Chapter 8

Continually Learning

I've discussed the part that mental stretching plays in keeping you young. But an added dimension to this is to continuously be learning something new. You should have a goal to learn something new each day at the very least no matter how small it is. And if you really want to capitalize on this idea you should maintain a list of "learning projects" as I do. You may even want to keep a journal of new and interesting things you've learned and set some goals as to what levels you would like to achieve in all these learning areas.

As an example, in my own situation I am currently working on becoming more knowledgeable about WW2, the Erie Canal, Florida history, IPAD capabilities, religions of the world, and growing roses. How's that for diversity? And diversity is a good thing to keep in mind as you identify new learning possibilities. Yes, it's okay to be learning more about those things you're pretty good at now. But launching yourself into some things that are totally new to you may be even more valuable. A friend of mine who had no musical experience decided to learn to play the saxophone when he retired. Maybe a musical instrument is in your future. And always remember the old adage, *"Everything I know is a result of my ignorance"*. Are there some things that you are ignorant about right now that you would like to know more about?

Writing is one of the best forms of learning. My writing of this book is a great example of this. I started with just a few ideas of things we could do expand our lives. The more I wrote about it the more ideas came to me. And, besides that, it opened up another whole new learning experience for me - learning the process of Kindle booklet writing and publishing.

Another aspect of the learning process is that of "unlearning" which may actually be more difficult than learning. It's been said that *"to gain knowledge you should learn something every day – to gain wisdom you should get rid of something every day".* If you are keeping a journal of your learning experiences you may want to add a section of things you've unlearned as well.

Sometimes learning can be as simple as wandering around and connecting with things. There is an old saying that "all who wander aren't lost". Wandering can be physical or mental and here are some examples of each:

Physical:

> Take walks in totally different places and observe everything you can. Look for the simple things around you and try to really get inside them. Look at *common* items and try to make them *uncommon*.

> Spend time watching birds or other animals and try to focus on their behaviors. Nature always supplies some great learning experiences.

> Do some people watching and study the behaviors of these rather strange animals.

> Wander through a bookstore and scan through as many books as you can – especially those that are really different.

Mental:

> Google something every day. Start by *Googling* yourself and you may be surprised at what comes up.

> Roam around Wikipedia or just select random pages and learn what you can.

> Walk through the dictionary – learn a new word each day.

Read a book about some topic that you have never imagined even thinking about.

Take time each day to observe the miracles that surround you.

Albert Einstein once said,

"There are two ways to live your life. One is as though nothing is a miracle. The other is though everything is a miracle."

Some of you may be very familiar with the devices and the plethora of information available to us these days – and some may not. There is a whole new world of discovery via the internet and all you have to do is a little searching. If you just have a word to describe an interest of yours you can simply Google it or used a number of other search engines (Bing, Yahoo, Ask.com, duckduck, etc) and see what comes up. Many of today's smart phones have the ability to verbally ask questions. If you own one of these, ask your smart phone a few questions today.

A number of colleges and communities have recognized the value of continued learning for those in their mature years. I live in a place called The Villages in Central Florida. They have a College of Lifelong Learning that offers courses and lectures in hundreds of topics. There are no tests, grades or pressure – just fun. If you Google "lifetime learning" or "continuing education" you will find numerous opportunities available from colleges and other learning institutions in your area. These are generally offered at an attractive cost and provide a great opportunity to learn new things.

ITunes U is an amazing source of free lectures and videos from various universities and learning institutions. I personally have a bookshelf of courses on the history of the US, the photographic history of rock and roll, jazz insights, frontiers of science innovation, cooking, gardening, and the music of Christopher Parkening as well as a few others.

Again, go for variety and a good mix between expanding your knowledge of things you now know and things you know nothing about. I even toyed with downloading a course on calculus (which was my favorite course in college) but then I asked, why? I try to spend at least a night a week listening to some of these lectures. You know what? You **can** teach old dogs new tricks! An IPod or similar device is an ideal vehicle for downloading although you can also download them to a PC, MAC, or laptop. It's just more difficult to curl up in bed reading your PC.

I have also started a process of learning at least one new word a day. I must admit that this is fun, even though I will likely forget most of these words in the near future due to lack of use. Try the *dictionary.com* App which supplies you with a new word every day along with a thesaurus, a rhyming dictionary, and a number of other "word goodies".

One other thought about learning. As I've mentioned before, a few years back I lost my first wife, Jan, to ovarian cancer. We were together for 40 years and the loss was devastating to me. One of the things I did to deal with this loss was to turn it into a learning experience and write a book about how to deal with the loss of a spouse, *Jan's Rainbow; Stories of Hope: How Those You Have Loved and Lost Stay in Touch With You*. This has just been published as a paperback and Kindle/Nook book under a new title, *Surviving the Loss of Your Loved One; Jan's Rainbow*. Writing this book had a huge impact on my own recovery bolstered by the fact that I was able to help so many others by doing this. So another thought for you is to turn negative experiences into learning experiences if you can.

Questions for **Chapter 8**

What are some things that you are curious about?

What are some specific topics you would like to know more about

What learning opportunities are available in your area?

Are there some negative experiences in your life that you can turn into learning experiences?

Chapter 9

Take Time out Each Day for Some "Dumb Stuff"

We need to reserve some time for doing things that have perhaps no redeeming value whatsoever other than to take us away from reality for a spell. If you like to spend time on your computer you may want to cruise around sites like *dumb.com* . This site offers a plethora of dumb things to do including dumb facts, chatting with God, old time radio, funny bumper stickers, a virtual Voodoo doll to torture your friends, and even a virtual bubble wrap that could entertain you for hours. There are over 100 things to see and do here. Go there right now!

Or you could just *google* around using words like dumb, silly, stupid etc. You'll be amazed at what you find. If reading is your thing go pick up some marginally useless books generally found in the humor section. Take some time away from "War and Peace" to peruse these dumb books.

 Ones I particularly like are cartoons like *The Far Side* and *Quigmans*. *The Book of Stupid Questions* by Tom Weller also comes to mind as does the *Imponderables Collection* of David Feldman (Why Do Clocks Run Clockwise?) And any book by David Barry is worth keeping around for those times when you really need to get the cobwebs out of your head. His best are *Babies and Other Hazards of Sex, Stay Fit and Healthy Until You're Dead*, and *Claw Your Way to the Top of the Organization*. For visual stimulation of dumb stuff there is nothing better than reruns of *Monty Python's Flying Circus*. You also might want to take some time to just do dumb things as well such as:

> Call Dial-A-Prayer and argue with them.

> Walk or drive backwards through a drive-up window.

Grow a beard (men only please) that will undoubtedly make you look older (ala Santa Claus). Then shave it off to take years off your life.

Get a coloring book and have at it.

Have a serious conversation with your dog or cat (or your neighbor's pet if you don't have one of your own).

Try "doodling". I know I'm dating myself but there was a time when doodling was the rage. It involves drawing what comes to mind. Get a pencil and a sketch pad and let your thoughts flow.

Wander around YouTube. You'd be amazed at how much is there and a lot of it is really dumb.

See the Appendix 5 for some more opportunities.

I wouldn't classify this as dumb stuff but I find that just spending time listening to some music (without anything else going on) can be very stimulating. I like almost all forms of music but especially classical and jazz. Find a comfortable chair, put on the earphones and just immerse yourself in some great piece of music for while and see what happens.

In Appendix 7 I've included some of the more interesting and entertaining facts that I've collected over the years. Spend a little time wandering through these when you get a chance. I think you will find them interesting and it'll definitely tickle your thinking.

As an aside, let me mention one of the clubs in The Villages called, *The Village Idiots*. I'm not sure how this one got started but I think it's a great idea. You may want to start a similar club of your own. The stated purpose of this club is that "they have no redeeming value whatsoever.

I could go on and on here because I've done a lot of marginally dumb things in my life. A few years ago I wrote a book called **Get Out of Your**

Thinking Box; 365 Ways To Brighten Your Life and Enhance Your Creativity. In it you will find a whole pile of things to do to tweak your thinking and tickle your funny bone. I've included a number of these ideas in Appendix 5.

Questions for **Chapter 9**

When is the last time you just let your mind wander? Did you enjoy the trip?

What are some of the dumbest things you've done in your life and how did you feel about them?

What are the 3 things on Dumb.com that you liked best?

What do you find when you Google stupid, dumb, and silly?

Chapter 10
Loving a Lot and Connecting With Your Friends

Does love really make the world go around? Maybe not, but it sure makes the world a better place to live. While on a speaking engagement in South Africa I became aware of one of the most interesting concepts ever. That concept is **Ubuntu.** The dictionary defines this as the quality made up of sympathy, kindness, and respect toward other people that is considered to be a part of the African way of life.

In Archbishop Desmond Tutu's words:

> *"A person with Ubuntu is open and available to others, affirming of others, does not feel threatened that others are able and good, based from a proper self-assurance that comes from knowing that he or she belongs in a greater whole and is diminished when others are humiliated or diminished, when others are tortured or oppressed".*

Other words that encompass this concept are, caring, trust, unselfishness, sharing, and curiosity. The concept of *ubuntu* is that a person is a person because of other people. I don't even exist until I'm acknowledged by others. Another way of putting this is "I am what I am because of who we all are". With that in mind, the quality of your life is intrinsically connected with the relations you have with other people. Look up *ubuntu* in Wikipedia and while you're there listen to the short video of Nelson Mandela explaining the concept. I guarantee this will have an impact on how you relate to those around you.

When I lost my wife, Jan, I was totally devastated and at times wasn't sure that I even wanted to live anymore. She was my high school sweetheart, my lover, the mother of our children, and my best friend and we had shared our lives for over 40 years. There was a sudden overwhelming emptiness in my life. Sure, I had a lot of friends and still had my kids (who all lived far away from me). The best decision I ever made was to become a part of a bereavement group which gave me the opportunity to share my feelings and experiences with others who had also lost spouses. Like they say, your best friends are those you meet in the *foxhole* and I was one lucky guy to meet my current wife who I believe saved my life with her love. This whole experience taught me the value that love plays in your life.

Don't be afraid to tell your spouse, children, grandchildren, family and friends that you love them. And don't be afraid to fall in love with them a little more each day. Laugh with them as much as you can. As Victor Borge says, *"Laughter is the shortest distance between two people."* And don't be afraid to cry with them as well in circumstances that call for it. If you have pets show them as much love as you can – they always eat that up. And a wagging tail or soft purr is a great stress reducer. And don't be afraid to show some affection to those you interact with each day even if it is just giving them a nice smile and wishing them a good day. Smiling at total strangers can make you both feel good. And don't worry about the one out of every hundred who may consider you a pervert.

Hugging is a great way to solidify relationships. Never pass up an opportunity to hug family and friends. You might be surprised how much most people enjoy a good hug. I think that among those who love to be hugged are nurses. I have an incredible respect for nurses and will always hug any nurse that assists me to show my appreciation.

I also never pass up an opportunity to shake the hand of a service man or women in the airport or any place else that I happen to spot them. And I always tell them, "Thanks for your service." I know it makes them feel good but it also makes me feel great. We can never show enough appreciation to those who serve their country. And while you are at it you might want to consider thanking a police officer, fire fighter, EMT or teacher. Some of these people put their lives on the line every day for you.

Extend a hand and help others out whenever you can, even if they are total strangers. If you are able, look into ways you can volunteer your time to helping others. While you're at it call up some of your old friends and tell them you've been thinking about them. Times flies and it is very easy to lose touch with old friends. Don't let that happen. Try to get in touch with an old friend at least once a week. Also, go out of your way to keep your relationships with family members no matter how far away they are.

Surround yourself with things you love (music, plants, pictures, keepsakes, hobbies etc.). This will help you to continually stay connected to those things that are important in your life.

Life is too short to waste on hating anyone or anything. I believe that most of us have built up fairly long lists of things or people that we dislike. As a matter of fact, many of our world problems exist because of long-standing biases and hatred that some have towards other people. Religions which should be based on our love for each other and mankind in general are sometimes sources of hatred instead. Witness what is going on in the Middle East and other parts of the world right now.

Try to make friends with someone who you have not cared for in the past. It may not always work but, if it helps you create a new friend, it will make you feel good. There is a double benefit here – you get the plus from creating a new friend and you eliminate a minus that you may have been carrying around for a while.

You may need to do some deep thinking to unveil some of the negative thoughts you are carrying around about certain people and things. We sometimes tend to hide these things away and refuse to recognize them. Make a list of all those things that instill negative thoughts in you no matter how insignificant you first think they are. Then rate them in terms of their potential impact on your life and begin a process of brainstorming things you can do to turn your feelings toward them into positive ones. Remember, the object is to bring more love into your life – and getting rid of some of your dislikes and biases that might be blocking your ability to show love will help you towards that end.

"Being deeply loved by someone gives you strength, while loving someone deeply gives you courage."
Lao Tzu

"Where there is love there is life."
Mahatma Gandhi

Questions for Chapter 10

Do you consider yourself a lovable person? Why/ Why not?

How do you express your love and admiration to your friends and family?

Who have you hugged lately? When did you last tell someone you love them?

When is the last time you lent a helping hand to someone? In what ways could you do this in the future?

Are their some friends from your past who you would like to reconnect with?

Are there some members of your family that you would like to reconnect with?

Are there things or people in your life that give you a negative feeling? What can you do about it?

Do your surroundings inspire your ability to love and give you positive feelings? If not, how might you change this?

Have you thanked someone for their service lately?

Chapter 11

Clean House

Remember the nice feeling that would always follow when you cleaned out the garage, attic or cellar? As you grow older it's important to clean out the "garages of your life" and keep them clean. We sometimes think of this as downsizing. Get rid of anything that isn't useful, beautiful, or joyful to you. There is stuff all around us, stuff in our heads, and, for those who spend a lot of time in the digital world, stuff in our computer files. A good metaphor for this whole process is the reconfiguration and defragmentation of computer drives. Every time I do this I feel better for some reason. Sometimes we just need to defragment our minds.

Cleaning house may involve going through attics, cellars, and closets and weeding out things you no longer need. Sometimes it turns out to be a very interesting discovery of photographs and artifacts from the past which you can pass on to various family members often with the effect of opening up nice conversations about times past. Isn't that better than having them going through all that stuff after you're gone? Sometimes it can result in a project of selling these items on EBay or other sites which may provide new opportunities for you. These are great side benefits of the process.

Cleaning house may also involve getting rid of some of the baggage you are carrying around in your head as well. What are some of your thoughts, biases, opinions, etc that are no longer valuable to you, or even result in negative forces in your life? It may be difficult if these have been hanging around for a while to cast them aside – but give it a try. You may find it makes a big difference in your outlook on life.

For those in their golden years it is important to make sure that those loved ones who you leave behind are not left dangling. Obviously having a will is of utmost importance. And I'm going to go out on the limb a bit and suggest that a large majority of us either don't have a will or have one that is outdated. A lot of folks move to friendlier climates when they retire without realizing that a will from one state may not be applicable in another state. Without a will your family might be subjected to some vultures that are waiting to get a piece of your estate – and I'm sure you wouldn't want to have that happen. If you have shied away from doing this because of the perceived cost there are a number of websites and some very inexpensive software available. One I have found to be very easy and friendly is <u>Will Maker</u>. You may also want to <u>try LegalZoom.com</u>.

Writing about this reminds me of a story I heard recently about an elderly gentleman who had a hearing problem. He finally decided to get some hearing aids and was pleasantly surprised that he could hear all the conversations that went on within his family. His doctor asked him how his family felt about how he could finally hear their conversations. His comment was, "I haven't told them I can hear them yet and I've changed my will 3 times already".

A few years ago I put together a document entitled ***When I Buy the Farm***. These are my own words without any legalese (as if I were capable of this) of what I would like to see happen when I'm gone. What are the things you would like to tell your family and friends if you could come back for a spell after your passing? Since you likely won't have the opportunity to do this, why not do it now in writing? And one advantage of this is that nobody will be able to argue with you.

Questions for Chapter 11

What are the things in your life that are useful, joyful, or beautiful to you?

Are their parts of your physical environment (attic, garage, closets, and storage spaces) that you haven't cleaned out in a while?

Do you have a will? Is it up to date?

What would you want to tell your family and friends when you pass on?

Chapter 12

Follow Your Spiritual Beliefs

And last but certainly not least!

This may be one the most important things you do to maintain a long, healthy life. As a matter of fact some of you may be thinking that I haven't even mentioned anything about the spiritual aspect of your lives. The importance of this is rather obvious but each of us has different ways of bringing this into our lives. Whatever your religion might be (Protestant, Catholic, Mormon, Jewish, Muslim or other) you need to recognize that there is a higher power that should be in your thoughts. Even agnostics and atheists need to have some spirituality in their lives. I'm not a preacher so that's all I'm going to say on this topic.

That's a pretty good start. You may be really tempted to just put this book down and go on with your life. Don't do it! Go back and try some of these things out. See if they add some zest to your life. And stop worrying. Remember, tomorrow is the just the today you worried about yesterday. And, besides that, the older you get the more those younger people think you are cute.

 I hope you enjoyed reading this as much as I enjoyed writing it. Please, please, **please write a review** if you can. I am also available to speak to groups in certain areas about this, and several other topics. I can be reached at lindsaycollier@comcast.net and also on Facebook, Linkedin, and Google+. Also, I'd be happy to send you my speaking brochure upon request.

 I'd love to hear from you regarding your experience using some of the ideas in this booklet as well as any thoughts you might have about other things that can be done to achieve a long, happy life.

Have fun growing young - Lindsay

Appendix 1 – Happy Words

Here are some happy words to get your started. Try to use these in your every day conversations. Replace any sad words you feel coming on with these. See how good it makes you feel and notice the positive impact it has on people you talk with.

Accomplished	Bubbly	Creative
Adored	Buoyant	Decent
Affectionate	Calm	Delighted
Agreeable	Caringly	Delightful
Alive	Celebratory	Determined
Altruistic	Charmed	Dignified
Amazed	Cheerful	Distinguished
Animated	Cheery	Dotingly
Beautiful	Chipper	Ducky
Blameless	Chirpy	Ebullient
Blessed	Comfortable	Ecstatic
Blissful	Confident	Effervescent
Bouncy	Content	Elated
Brave	Contented	Endeared
Brilliant	Contentment	Energetic

Enjoyable

Enlightened

Enthusiastic

Entrusted

Euphoric

Excellent

Exceptional

Excited

Extraordinary

Exuberant

Exultant

Fabulous

Fantabulous

Fantastic

Festive

First-class

First-rate

Flattered

Fondly

Fortunate

Friendly

Fulfillment

Full of beans

Full of brio

Full of joie de vivre

Full of life

Fun-loving

Gallant

Giddy

Giggly

Glad

Gleeful

Good

Good-humored

Grateful

Gratification

Great

Greetings

Happiness

Happy

Harmonious

Heart warming

Heavenly

Helpful

High-spirited

Honest

Honorable

Honored

Hopeful

Idyllic

Impressed

In high spirits

Inspired

Invigorated

Jolly

Jovial

Joy

Joyful

Joyous

Jubilant

Just	Kind	Liking
Lively	Merry	Playful
Lofty	Noble	Pleasant
Loved	On cloud nine	Pleased
Lovely	Optimistic	Pleasurable
Lovingly	Outstanding	Pleasure
Loyal	Overjoyed	Privileged
Magnificent	Peaceful	Productive
Marvelous	Perfect	Quality
Recharged	Satisfied	
Re-energized	Smitten	Thrilled
Refreshed	Special	Tickled
Rejuvenated	Spectacular	Touched
Relaxed	Spirited	Tranquil
Respectable	Stoked	Tremendous
Revitalized	Successful	Triumphant
Revived	Superb	Uplifting
Righteous	Sweet	Victorious
Romantic	Tenderly	Virtuous
Satisfaction	Thankful	Vivacious

Warm hearted	Well	Wonderful
Wholeheartedl	Wonder struck	

Appendix 2 - Some Titles you may want to give yourself

Remember – you are the boss of you. Feel better about yourself by taking on your own personal title. Here are some examples.

- Chief Gadfly

- Sorcerer's Apprentice

- Purveyor of Outrageously Interesting Ideas

- Rattler of Bushes

- Ruffler of Feathers

- Keeper of Pit Bulls for Mouth Foaming Creativity

- Zen Cat

- Purveyor of Feet in the Backside

- Slayer of Sacred Cows

- Mistress of Chaos

- Royal Stardust Keeper

- Yah-Butt Blaster

- Supreme Allied Commander

- Mind Mine Sweeper

- Supreme Strategic Processtologist

- Catcher of All That Hits Fans

- Wild Thing
- Sand Box Monitor
- Heel Nipper
- Happily Ever After Maker
- Empress of the Universe
- Resident Disturber of the Peace
- Raging Inexorable Thunder-Lizard Evangelist
- Wild thing
- Supreme Allied Commander
- All That Is Powerful and Wise
- Big Kahuna
- Muckety Muck
- Duchess of Danger
- Troublemaker
- Director of Fun
- Resultant
- Master of Madness
- Vibe Evolver
- Pride Piper of Creativity
- Wicker Good Idea Generator
- Idea Steward
- Idea Gooser
- Chief Creatologist

- Myth Debunker

- Resident Dreamer

- Seer, Inspirer, and Spark Plug

- Wizard of Wonder

- Resident Disturber of the Peace

- Hope Builder

- Liberator of Fools

- Super Simplifier

- Cerebral proctologist

- Innovation Evangelist

- Chief Imagination Officer

- Insight Manager

- Human Being

- Control Czar

- Director of Everything

- Chief Humor Officer

- Squeezer of Thinking Juices

- Manager of Mischief

- Resultant

Appendix 3 – Some Quotations to Tickle Your Brain

Here are a few quotations to help influence your thinking. For a complete look at all my favorite quotations check out my book, **Quotations to Tickle Your Brain** available in both paperback and Kindle version.

1. It's never too late to have a happy childhood.

2. You are only young once - but you can be immature all your life.

3. Don't be afraid to take a big step if it's needed. You can't cross a chasm in two small jumps.

4. Life is like being on a dog sled team. If you ain't the lead dog the scenery never changes.

5. A diamond is just a piece of coal that stuck to the job.

6. If in the last few years you haven't discarded a major opinion or acquired a new one then check your pulse - you may be dead.

7. Once you have taken the impossible into your calculations, its possibilities become potentially limitless.

8. You can't always depend on expert opinion. A turkey, if you ask the turkey, should be stuffed with grasshoppers, grit and worms.

9. The road to success is always under construction.

10. Do not take life too seriously - you will never get out of it alive.

11. To know what to ask is already to know half. (Aristotle)

12. Carve a person's faults in sand, their accomplishments in stone.

13. If the roof doesn't leak, the architect hasn't been creative enough. (Frank Lloyd Wright)

14. Once a new technology runs over you, you are not part of the steamroller; you are part of the road.

15. It's better to build a fence at the top of the cliff than a hospital at the bottom. (Ann Landers)

16. The best way to predict the future is to invent it. (Alan Kay)

17. You can't build a reputation on what you're going to do. (Henry Ford)

18. Verbal diarrhea is created by people who make vowel movements consonantly.

19. If you torture data sufficiently, it will confess to anything. (Fred Menger)

20. Optimists see an opportunity in every problem. Pessimists see a problem in every opportunity.

21. Seek simplicity - then distrust it. (Alfred North Whitehead)

22. Everywhere you trip is where the treasure lies. (Warren Bennis)

23. If we think more about failing at what we are doing than about doing it, we will not succeed. (Warren Bennis)

24. Everything should be made as simple as possible, but not simpler. (Albert Einstein)

25. The winner sees a green near every sand trap. The loser sees a sand trap near every green.

26. The world that we have made, as a result of the level of thinking we have done thus far, creates problems that we cannot solve at the same level at which we create them. (Albert Einstein)

27. The things that got you to where you are today are not the things that will get you to the future. (Peter Drucker)

28. Conception is easier than birth - and a good deal more pleasant too.

29. Never underestimate the unimportance of everything. (Steve Allen Jr.)

30. No great idea ever entered the mind through the mouth.

31. Be what you is, not what you ain't - cause if you is what you ain't, you ain't what you is. (Luther D. Price -jazz musician)

32. People who are always raising the roof usually don't have much in the attic.

33. A river is like intelligence - the deeper it is the less noise it makes.

34. No snowflake in an avalanche feels responsible.

35. A ship in harbor is safe - but that is not what ships are for. (John Shedd)

36. It usually takes me at least 3 weeks to prepare a good impromptu speech. (Mark Twain)

37. Only mediocre people are always at their best. (Somerset Maugham)

38. Intelligent people, when assembled into an organization, will tend toward collective stupidity. (Karl Albrecht)

39. Nothing would be done at all if a man waited until he could do it so well that no one could find fault with it. (Cardinal Newman)

40. When in doubt, I tell the truth. (Mark Twain)

41. A vision without a task is but a dream, a task without a vision is drudgery, a vision and a task is the hope of the world. (1730, a church in Sussex England)

42. Anyone who can spell a word only one way is an idiot. (WC Fields)

43. An optimist sees an opportunity in every calamity; a pessimist sees a calamity in every opportunity.

44. Some people never hear opportunity knock because they are too busy knocking opportunity. (Hal Chadwick)

45. What great thing would you attempt if you knew you could not fail. (Robert Schuler)

46. Just because everything is changed doesn't mean anything is different. (Alfred E. Neuman)

47. It is difficult to predict, especially about the future. (Peter Drucker)

48. Do not fear mistakes, there are none. (Miles Davis)

49. Good judgment comes from experience, experience comes from bad judgment. (Tom Watson - IBM)

50. Businesses 3 worst enemies are thinking too big, thinking too small and thinking too much.

51. It takes a long time to grow young. (Picasso)

52. You miss 100% of the shots you don't take. (Wayne Gretsky)

53. I skate to where the puck is going to be, not to where it is. (Wayne Gretsky)

54. Things may come to those who wait, but only the things left by those who hustle. (Abraham Lincoln)

55. Think left and think right and think low and think high. Oh the thinks you can think up if only you try. (Dr. Seuss)

56. A bird does not sing because it has an answer. It sings because it has a song. - Yurok Indian

57. When your heart speaks take good notes. (Yurok Indian)

58. Angels can fly because they take themselves lightly.

59. If the earth had waited for a precedent, it never would have turned on its axis. (Maria Mitchell, astronomer)

60. You are only as good as you dare to be bad. (Timothy Hutton)

61. You can really see a lot by observing. (Yogi Berra)

62. To create you must first destroy. (Picasso)

63. Any significantly advantaged technology is indistinguishable from magic.

64. Next time your mind wanders follow it around for a while. (Lindsay Collier)

65. A new idea is first condemned as ridiculous and then dismissed as trivial, until finally it becomes what everyone knows. (William James)

66. Faced with the choice between changing one's mind and proving there is no need to do so, most people get busy on the proof. (J.K. Galbraith)

67. If I give you a dollar and you give me a dollar we each have a dollar. If I give you an idea and you give me an idea we each have two ideas.

68. Two roads diverged in the wood and I took the one less traveled by, and that has made all the difference. (Robert Frost)

69. Get your facts first, then you can distort them as much as you please. (Mark Twain)

70. If you lose the power to laugh you lose the power to think. (Clarence Darrow)

71. If you have always done it that way, it is probably wrong. (Charles Kettering)

72. Things will get better - despite our efforts to improve them. (Will Rogers)

73. If the parts don't fit the theory - change the theory. (Albert Einstein)

74. Learn the infield fly rule. This will give you a good perspective on life. (Forest Gump)

75. If you think you're too small to be effective you have never been in bed with a mosquito. (Bette Reese)

76. In order to make an omelet you have to break a few eggs.

77. Sometime trying to tune up the old engine is like putting lipstick on a pig. (EDS executive)

78. In the race to the future there are passengers, drivers, and road kill. (C.K. Prahalad)

79. Organizational change is like dancing with a gorilla. You don't stop when you get tired, you stop when the gorilla gets tired.

80. When one door closes, another one opens somewhere.

81. Not everything that matters can be measured, and not everything that can be measured matters. (Albert Einstein)

82. If you don't change your direction you'll likely end up where you're going. (Chinese proverb)

83. Be the change you are trying to create. (Gandhi)

84. You usually don't drown in the sea, you drown in a puddle.

85. Anyone who thinks they're indispensable should stick a finger in a bowl of water and notice the hole it leaves when it's pulled out. (Harvey Mackay)

86. Nothing is less productive than to make more efficient what should not be done at all. (Peter Drucker)

87. Every right idea, no matter how good it is, is eventually the wrong idea. (Peter Drucker)

88. A cow chip is a picnic to a fly. (Texas Bix Bender)

89. We're all in this alone. (Lily Tomlin)

90. Thunder is good. Thunder is impressive. But it's the lightning that does the work. (Mark Twain)

91. Better to remain silent and be thought a fool than to speak up and remove all doubt. (Abraham Lincoln)

92. Reality is for people who lack imagination. - seen on a bumper sticker

93. I am not young enough to know everything. (Little Zen Companion)

94. Whether you believe you can or believe you can't, you're absolutely right. (Henry Ford)

95. The "silly question" is the first intimation of some totally new development. (Alfred North Whithead)

96. Many ideas grow better when transplanted into another mind than in the one where they sprung up. (Oliver Wendell Holmes)

97. When companies try to encourage creativity it's like a bear dancing with an ant. Sooner or later the ant will realize it's a bad idea, although the bear might not. (Scott Adams -Dilbert)

98. Every great oak was once a nut that stood its ground.

99. Managers can't demand creativity any more than they can order growth from a flower. (John Kao)

Appendix 4 – Tips for Being Creative

Here are 10 things you can do to be creative all the time.

1. Create a stretch vision of what you want.

2. Try your best to be non-judgmental.

3. Start from outrageous and work back. Practice mental bungie jumping.

4. Examine and upset your thinking patterns often.

5. Break the rules.

6. Seek advice from others - especially those outside your expertise.

7. Wonder a lot and let your ideas and thoughts marinate.

8. If at first you don't succeed - give up - let go.

9. Think in metaphors as much as you can.

10. Laugh a lot and never lose touch with your sense of humor.

11.

Appendix 5 – A Few Dumb Things You Can Do

(From my book, *Get Out of Your Thinking Box; 365 Ways to Brighten Your Life and Enhance Your Creativity*)

1. Call a random number and just wish someone a nice day.
2. Look at the world as if your eyes were on your knee caps.
3. Have a "whine and Jeez" party.
4. Come up with a nonsense language and use it with your friends.
5. Listen to some old time radio shows (dumb.com).
6. Go to a bank and ask for change for a nickel.
7. Think of all the ways your life is like a *slinky*.
8. Go skip rocks on a pond.
9. Go test drive an 18 wheeler.
10. Wear a silly hat all day.
11. Spell check all your friends names and see what comes up. One of my friends' names came up as "cheery hormones".
12. Interview some people telling them you are writing a book on some strange topic.
13. Carry out a conversation with someone as if you are an opera singer.
14. Pretend you are a sponge for a day and soak up everything you can. Wring yourself out at the end of the day. If your name is 'Bob" skip this one.
15. Tap dance.
16. Write down all the things that are bothering you on a roll of toilet paper – and flush it.
17. Try your best to be dyslexic for a day.
18. Think of some things that you've never thought about before.
19. Build a model (plane, car, rocket etc.).
20. Visit a cemetery and read the epitaphs.
21. Create your own personal logo.
22. Try to have a serious conversation with your dog or cat.

23. Build a house of cards.
24. Think of as many stupid questions as you can (even though there is no such thing as a stupid question).
25. Browse through a library.
26. Read a Dr. Seuss book.
27. View the world from the perspective of an insect.
28. Read a book of quotations. Start with my book, **Quotations to Tickle Your Brain**.
29. Spend 15 minutes belly laughing for no reason at all.
30. Pick a few objects around you and try to see what it would be like to be those objects.

Appendix 6 – Some Interesting Facts to Stimulate Your Thinking

Need something to do in the wandering zone. Just play a bit with these facts.

1. You're in Paris and you decide to use your AMEX. Getting credit approval involves a 46,000
mile journey over phones and computers. The job is done in 5 seconds! - Peter Large, Micro Revolution Revisited

2. The EINIAC, commonly thought of as the first modern computer, was built in 1944. It took up more space than an 18-wheeler's tractor-trailer, weighed more than 17 Chevrolet Camaros, and consumed 140,000 watts of electricity. Einiac could execute up to 5,000 basic arithmetic operations per second.

3. One of today's popular microprocessors, the 486, is built on a tiny piece of silicon about the size of a dime. It weighs less than a packet of sweet and low, and uses less than 2 watts of electricity. A 486 can execute up to 54,000,000 instructions per second!

4. Computer power is now 8,000 times less expensive than it was 30 years ago. If we had similar progress in automotive technology, today you could buy a Lexus for about $2. It would travel at the speed of sound, and go about 600 miles on a thimble of gas. - John Naisbitt, Global Paradox

5. At the rate of one execution per day, it would take seven years to execute everyone who is on death row in the United States.

6. The US has 70% of the world's lawyers, one per 335 people. In Japan the ratio is one per every 9000 people.

7. The nucleus accounts for almost all the atom's solidarity yet occupies one million millionth of its total volume. The rest is empty space (with electrons spinning around). Bodies are mostly empty space. The solid matter for all the human bodies on earth lumped together would be no bigger than a pea. The solid matter for the entire world would fit inside a football stadium!

8. The entire continent of Africa has fewer phones than the city of Tokyo.

9. Farmington, Maine is the Earmuff Capital of the World. Chester Greenwood invented them in 1873 at age 13.

10. The distance between the wing tips of a Boeing 747 is longer than the Wright Brothers' first flight.

11. In 1977, US carmakers actually recalled more vehicles than they produced.

12. If every fax owner switched to ½ page cover sheets instead of a full page, it would save nearly 2 million miles of un-recyclable fax paper annually.

13. Some natural shampoos and toothpastes are no different than industrial strength cleaners - they rely on detergents to break down grease. Unfortunately, detergents break down human cell walls as well and are thought by some to be carcinogenic.

14. Cushioned heels may be good for your body and soles, but shoes with leather uppers are laced with residual chromium. Worse, highly toxic lead accounts for 2 to 3% of the polyvinyl chloride used in the soles of some shoes.

15. Gas-guzzlers are harder on the environment than electric cars, right? Wrong! A conventional car creates 26 tons of hazardous waste for every ton the vehicle weighs. A battery-powered automobile produces twice as much 0 52 tons, including a witches' brew of lead and toxic acids.

16. Boob tubes contain more than 4,000 chemicals, some of which you inhale while watching (because of off-gassing). In addition, since each set contains 18-20 grams of toxic mercury, driving a truckload of TV's would qualify you as a toxic waste hauler.

17. Your favorite jeans may be 100% cotton, but that doesn't make them 100% pure. While cotton amounts to only 3% of the world's crops, its cultivation consumes 26% of the world's tonnage of pesticides.

18. No matter what their contents, aluminum cans can't be completely recycled into new aluminum cans - the recycled aluminum is too impure. So every year millions of pounds of hazardous slag are shipped to waste dumps in third world countries.

19. The combined wealth of the world's 358 billionaires now equals the total income of the poorest 45 percent of the world's population, some 2.3 billion people. (United *Nations' Human Development Report 1996*)

20. On a Canadian two-dollar bill the flag flying over the Parliament Building is an American flag.

21. Both diamond and graphite are composed of only carbon atoms, but because of different pattern, diamond is the hardest substance known and graphite is one of the softest.

22. The patent for the fax machine was issued 30 years before the telephone in 1843 and the first commercial fax was sent in 1865.

23. A nanometer is to a pebble as a pebble is to the earth's diameter.

24. Using 50 nanometer pits on a CD rather than the current size (10 square micrometers) would allow you to get the equivalent of 1000 CD's on the size of a wristwatch.

25. Let's say you're going to a party, so you pull out some pocket change and buy a little greeting card that plays "Happy Birthday" when it's opened. After the party, someone casually tosses the card into the trash, throwing away more computer power than existed in the entire world before 950.

26. No word in the English language rhymes with month, silver, orange, or purple.

27. The home video camera you use to take pictures contains more processing power than an old IBM 360, the wonder machine that gave birth to the mainframe computer age. And the Saturn system made by game maker, Sega, runs on a higher-performance processor than the original 1976 Cray supercomputer that in its day was accessible only to the most elite physicists.

28. The average vocabulary has 8000 words. The average supermarket has over 12,000 brands.

29. Peanuts are one of the ingredients of dynamite.

30. Rubber bands last longer when refrigerated.

31. Charly Chaplin once entered a Charly Chaplin look-alike contest and came in third!

32. Spiders' silk has long been used in the lenses of gun sites and surveying instruments. It is finer and stronger than anything made by man. One pound of spider web would stretch fifteen thousand miles.

33. Almonds are members of the peach family.

34. A dragonfly has a life span of 24 hours and a goldfish has a memory span of 3 seconds.

35. In England, the Speaker of the House is not allowed to speak.

36. A single pair of fruit flies in just one year can produce 700 to 800 offspring. Wow, that a lot of diapers!

37. An estimated 5 million trillion bacteria live on Earth and they have a combined weight roughly equal to the top 3 feet of France.

38. Ever wonder how big a trillion is? If you had a stack of one-thousand-dollar bills totaling $1 million in front of you it would be about 3 inches high. A billion dollars in one-thousand-dollar bills would reach about 250 feet. One trillion dollars would be a little over forty-seven miles high!

39. Two human eyes have more information processing capacity than all the supercomputers in the world.

40.

About the Author

Lindsay Collier presently resides in The Villages, Florida with his wife, Jean. After serving as a Captain in the US Army Corps of Engineers he joined Eastman Kodak as an engineer and took an early retirement after 25 years. During his tenure at Kodak he became their expert in creative thinking and innovation and went on to become an author, speaker and consultant after his retirement. He has shared his ideas with many organizations in the US and abroad in the form of books, workshops, and keynote presentations.

Lindsay is available for speaking engagements on the topic of this booklet as well as a number of other topics. His talks are chock full of great information along with some great humor. He can be contacted at lindsaycollier@comcast.net .

Other books by Lindsay Collier

amazon.com/author/lindsaycollier

Organizational Mental Floss; How to Squeeze Your Organization's Thinking Juices

Organizational Braindroppings; Musings on Organizational Breakthrough and Change

Quotations to Tickle Your Brain

Surviving Loss of A Loved One: Jan's Rainbow

Living Your Retirement Dreams and Growing Young in The Villages; Florida's Friendliest and Healthiest Hometown

The Whack-A-Mole Theory; Creating Breakthrough and Transformation in Organizations

Get Out of Your Thinking Box; 365 Ways to Brighten Your Life and Enhance Your Creativity

Jan's Rainbow; Stories of Hope; How Those You Have Lost Stay in Touch With You.

77317665R00062

Made in the USA
Columbia, SC
27 September 2017